Coming to America

Why Irish Immigrants Came to America

Lewis K. Parker

Rigby

Why Irish Immigrants Came to America
Copyright © 2002 by Rosen Book Works, Inc.

On Deck™ Reading Libraries
Published by Rigby
a division of Reed Elsevier Inc.
1000 Hart Road
Barrington, IL 60010-2627
www.rigby.com

Book Design: Mindy Liu and Erica Clendening
Text: Lewis K. Parker
Photo Credits: Cover, p. 19 © AP/Wide World Photos; p. 5 (top)
© MapArt; p. 5 (bottom) by courtesy of the Ellis Island Immigration
Museum; pp. 6, 7 © Hulton/Archive/Getty Images; p. 8 © Sean Sexton
Collection/Corbis; pp. 9, 21 Library of Congress, Prints and Photographs
Division; p. 10 General Research Division, The New York Public Library,
Astor, Lenox and Tilden Foundations; p. 11 © Bradford Art Galleries and
Museums, West Yorkshire, UK/Bridgeman Art Library; p. 12 Idaho Historical
Society, #1037-21; p. 13 photo by Benjamin F. Upton, Minnesota Historical
Society; p. 14 (inset) © Bettmann/Corbis; pp. 14–15 © Schenectady
Museum, Hall of Electrical History Foundation/Corbis; p. 17 courtesy
Museum of the City of New York, Clarence J. Davies Collection; p. 20
© Francine Fleischer/Corbis

On Deck™ is a trademark of Reed Elsevier Inc.

09 08 07 06
10 9 8 7 6 5 4 3

Printed in China

ISBN 0-7578-2460-9

Contents

Ireland and England

In the 1800s, Ireland was part of Great Britain, which was ruled by England. Irish people were not allowed to vote or own land. Many Irish people did not have jobs. Many of them wanted to find a better way of life.

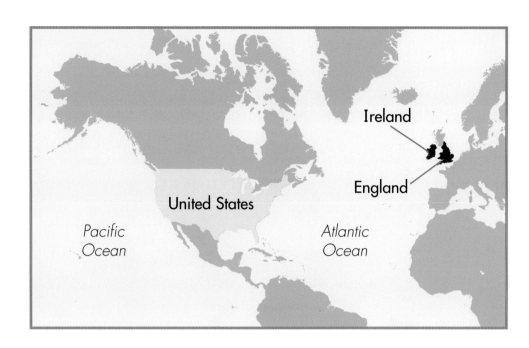

Ireland

England

United States

Pacific
Ocean

Atlantic
Ocean

Irish Servants.

JUST ARRIVED, *in the* Ship JOHN, *Capt.* ROACH,
from DUBLIN,
A NUMBER of HEALTHY, INDENTED
MEN and WOMEN SERVANTS :
AMONG THE FORMER ARE,
A Variety of TRADESMEN, with some good FAR-
MERS, and stout LABOURERS : Their Indentures will be disposed
of, on reasonable Terms, for CASH, by
GEORGE SALMON.
Baltimore, May 24, 1792.

This ad appeared in a Baltimore, Maryland,
newspaper in 1792. It says that Irish immigrants
who have just come to America are looking for jobs.

The Great Hunger

The potato was the most important food in Ireland. Many people in Ireland were potato farmers. Farmers rented the land they farmed from the British. They had to sell part of their potato crop to pay the rent.

Potatoes grow underground. They contain many vitamins and minerals. Irish male workers ate up to 14 pounds of potatoes a day.

In 1845, a plant disease destroyed Ireland's potato crop. Potatoes rotted in the ground or soon after they were gathered. The time from 1845 to 1851 was known as the Great Hunger.

Many farmers could not pay their rent during the Great Hunger. Many British who owned the land often made people leave their homes.

During the Great Hunger, many Irish people had no jobs. They did not have enough food to eat. Some people ate grass, seaweed, and dogs. Many people died. Others went to live in other countries. The number of people in Ireland dropped from about eight million people to about six million people.

Many people packed up all of their belongings and left Ireland during the Great Hunger.

During the Great Hunger, many Irish people did not eat every day.

The Fact Box

In April 1847, the USS *Jamestown* arrived in Ireland from Boston, Massachusetts. It carried 800 tons of food, supplies, and clothing to help the Irish people.

Coming to America

Almost one million Irish people moved to America during the Great Hunger. Irish immigrants came across the Atlantic Ocean in ships. The trip often took as long as ten weeks. Living conditions on the ships were very bad. Sometimes, as many as 900 people would be crowded below deck into a space that was planned for 30 or 40 people.

Irish immigrants often had to crowd below deck in small areas when they traveled to America.

Some Irish immigrants had their trip paid for by rich Americans. When these immigrants reached America, they worked as servants for the people who paid for their trip.

Most new immigrants in America had little money. Many men took low-paying and often unsafe jobs as laborers. They worked hard building roads, railroads, and canals. Some worked at putting down streetcar tracks or making sewers.

Many Irish immigrants made their living as miners. The work of a miner was very hard and unsafe.

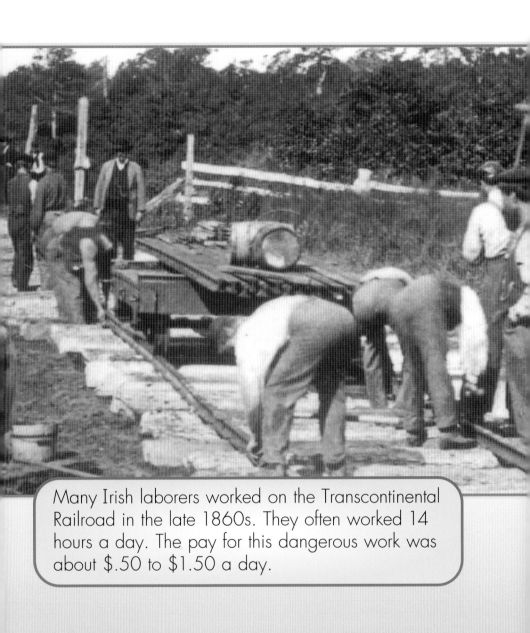

Many Irish laborers worked on the Transcontinental Railroad in the late 1860s. They often worked 14 hours a day. The pay for this dangerous work was about $.50 to $1.50 a day.

More Irish women than men came to America. Many women found jobs as maids or cooks. Others worked in factories.

Mary Harris Jones, also known as Mother Jones, was an Irish immigrant. She worked to get equal rights for coal miners and other workers.

Some Irish women worked in factories where they could earn six to ten cents for each piece of clothing they made. They worked 13 to 14 hours a day and could only make, at most, nine pieces of clothing a week.

Most Irish immigrants lived in large cities. The immigrants stayed together and formed their own neighborhoods. Some Americans didn't like the Irish immigrants. They thought that the Irish were taking jobs away from other Americans.

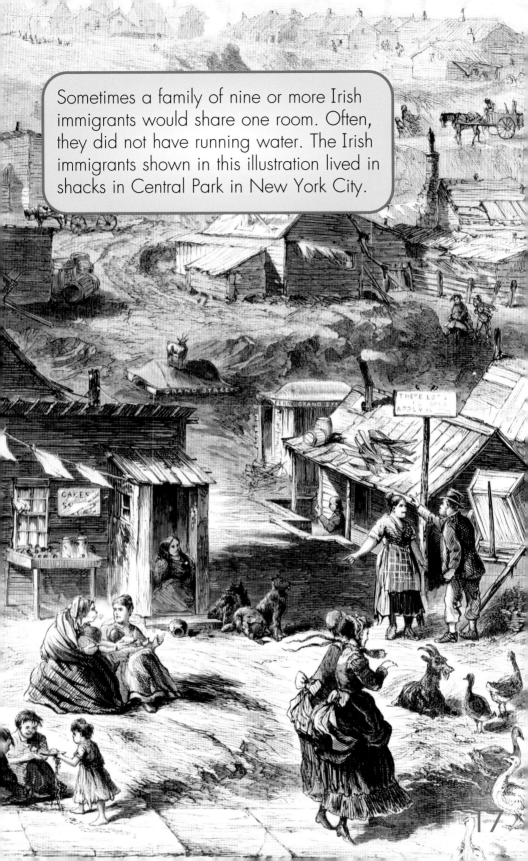

Sometimes a family of nine or more Irish immigrants would share one room. Often, they did not have running water. The Irish immigrants shown in this illustration lived in shacks in Central Park in New York City.

17

A New Life

By the late 1800s, more than three million Irish had come to America. In a short time, Irish immigrants had found a better way of life for themselves and their children.

The Fact Box

The oldest Irish American newspaper, the *Irish World*, was started in 1871.

BRICK TOWNSHIP HIGH SCHOOL
MARCHING ⚫ DRAGONS

St. Patrick is an important religious figure to many Irish people. Every year, millions of people enjoy the St. Patrick's Day Parade in New York City.

The Irish have been an important part of American life for more than 200 years. Irish Americans fought in the Revolutionary War and signed the Declaration of Independence. Irish immigrants have played an important part in the growth of America.

Frank McCourt is a famous Irish American author.

"America was Ireland's promised land, as it has been for so many other groups that have found hope and opportunity here and have made America great."

—Senator Edward Kennedy

Andrew Jackson was the son of Irish immigrants. He was elected the seventh president of the United States.

Glossary

canals (kuh-**nalz**) a large ditch dug between two places that boats can travel on

Declaration of Independence (dehk-luh-**ray**-shuhn **uhv** ihn-dih-**pehn**-duhns) the public statement made on July 4, 1776, in which America said it was free from England

disease (duh-**zeez**) illness

immigrant (**ihm**-uh-gruhnt) a person who comes into a country to live there

laborers (**lay**-buhr-uhrz) workers

religious (rih-**lihj**-uhs) having to do with a system of faith or belief

Revolutionary War (rehv-uh-**loo**-shuh-nehr-ee **wohr**) the war fought by the American colonies from 1775 to 1783 to be free from England's rule

Transcontinental Railroad (tran-skahn-tuh-**nehn**-tl **rayl**-rohd) a railroad system going across North America

Resources

Books
Irish Immigrants, 1840–1920
by Megan O'Hara
Capstone Press (2001)

The Irish American Family Album
by Dorothy and Thomas Hoobler
Oxford University Press Children's Books (1998)

Web Site
The Irish in America
http://www.pbs.org/wgbh/pages/irish

Index